The Church Board

Organized and Functioning

The Church Board

Organized and Functioning

by
Leon Chambers

Nazarene Publishing House
Kansas City, Missouri

First Printing, 1985
by Nazarene Publishing House

ISBN: 083-411-0822

Printed in the
United States of America

Cover: Royce Ratcliff

10 9 8 7 6 5 4 3 2 1

Contents

Foreword

I am pleased that this book is available for the use of pastors and church boards. I am glad for the expertise of the author and the suggestions that he presents which are workable and useful. A properly functioning church board brings satisfaction to the church board member in fulfillment of what is for him an assignment in the cause and the advancement of God's kingdom. It also provides a genesis for church growth. A well-functioning church board results in progressive ideas, successful achievement of programs, and a minimum of frictions arising within the church body itself. Any pastor who succeeds in operating a church board successfully for the advancement of the church will know an achievement himself and will deliver a better ministry to the people as he more and more is able to give attention to being the "shepherd of the flock" and the leader in evangelistic soul-winning advance.

—V. H. Lewis

Introduction

The purpose of this handbook on church board organization and functions is to assist the busy pastor in his effort to find more time for his major responsibilities: preaching and ministering to the needs of his people. An additional purpose is to give guidance to those laymen who have been elected to membership on the church board. They are, therefore, leaders of the church. They should be spiritual leaders: praying for the church, promoting evangelism, setting a Christian example, and, more than any other group in the church, assisting the pastor in exercising a spiritual watchcare over the entire congregation.

The Apostles, like the pastor, were faced with the problem of finding time for major responsibilities: "It is not reason that we should leave the word of God, and serve tables" (Acts 6:2). They found the answer: Spirit-filled laymen to carry out specified duties as well as give spiritual leadership. This is still the answer for a time-pressured ministry.

The first step in administration is to identify the tasks to be accomplished. Then it must be made clear to whom these specific duties will be entrusted and how they are to be carried out.

However, before this can be done, the pastor will be faced with several troublesome questions: Can others handle these duties? Will I lose control? Will I lose standing and recognition? Will I have time to train the committees?

Next, the pastor is faced with the need to evaluate honestly the above questions and consider the following. Few laymen have been trained to handle church duties, but they can be trained. Where there is organization, the pastor will gain in stature, receive added status as an administrator, and need fear no loss of control with the church board organized and functioning.

When the pastor feels that he has to supervise buildings, grounds, budgets, visitation, and the social life of the church in addition to his pulpit ministry, it is time to set his priorities in order and train laymen as helpers.

A few years ago, I made a survey of 31 church administrators, 100 pastors, and 100 laymen who were asked to list in sequence of importance the 10 factors that each considered the most important to the success of a minister. Good study habits was listed as number one by each group. Every laymen listed it. The pastor should make time for study a major priority. An organized and functioning church board will help to make this possible.

In the first few weeks of the local church year the pastor may feel that the time spent in training the church board is not worth the rewards. In due time, however, training will require very little time. As lay productivity increases as a result of training, the pastor will have more time for his specific duties. This handbook might serve as a basic guide for training sessions. Of course, additions and modifications can be made according to the needs of the individual churches.

In this handbook, committees have been identified, their organization has been explained, and their duties have been pointed out. Now it is a matter of training the elected personnel. I use this method: (1) tell them how; (2) show them how; and (3) let them try it. A word of caution is offered relative to the number of committees: Keep them to a minimum. A good rule to follow is never create a new committee if one in existence can do the job.

Motivation of the church board is important. This includes three things.

1. *Building confidence.* Let us assume that you are working with the chairman of the Board of Trustees. An

example of what might be said is: "Mr. John Doe, this entire church has elected you as a trustee, and the Board of Trustees elected you as chairman. The work of this board is of particular importance. It requires as chairman a person of mature judgment and one who will see after the Lord's property with as much care as he would give to his own. Their vote indicates and I too feel you are that kind of man."

2. *Making sure duties are understood.* This will be done by going over their duties with each committee and giving opportunity for questions.

3. *Reward.* One example is by reporting in the weekly newsletter work accomplished.

No committee should operate as an independent entity. Remember, the pastor is the president of the church organization and chairman of the church board. No committee can operate beyond the limits set by the church board and the *Manual.* If a pastor will always operate by the *Manual,* it will be his friend and protector in any crisis.

No pastor alone can build God's Church. It is only through men and women—specifically the church board— who have given themselves to Christ with a commitment as complete as the pastor's that this is done.

This church board handbook is based on the *Manual* of the Church of the Nazarene (1980 edition) and on my doctoral dissertation, "Task Identification and Analysis for Administration in the Church of the Nazarene." Changes and modification can be made for churches of varied sizes. I used this organizational structure in a church with less than 100 members and one with over 300 members.

I trust that God will make this handbook useful to pastor and board members as they work together to build their area of the Kingdom's work.

—Leon Chambers

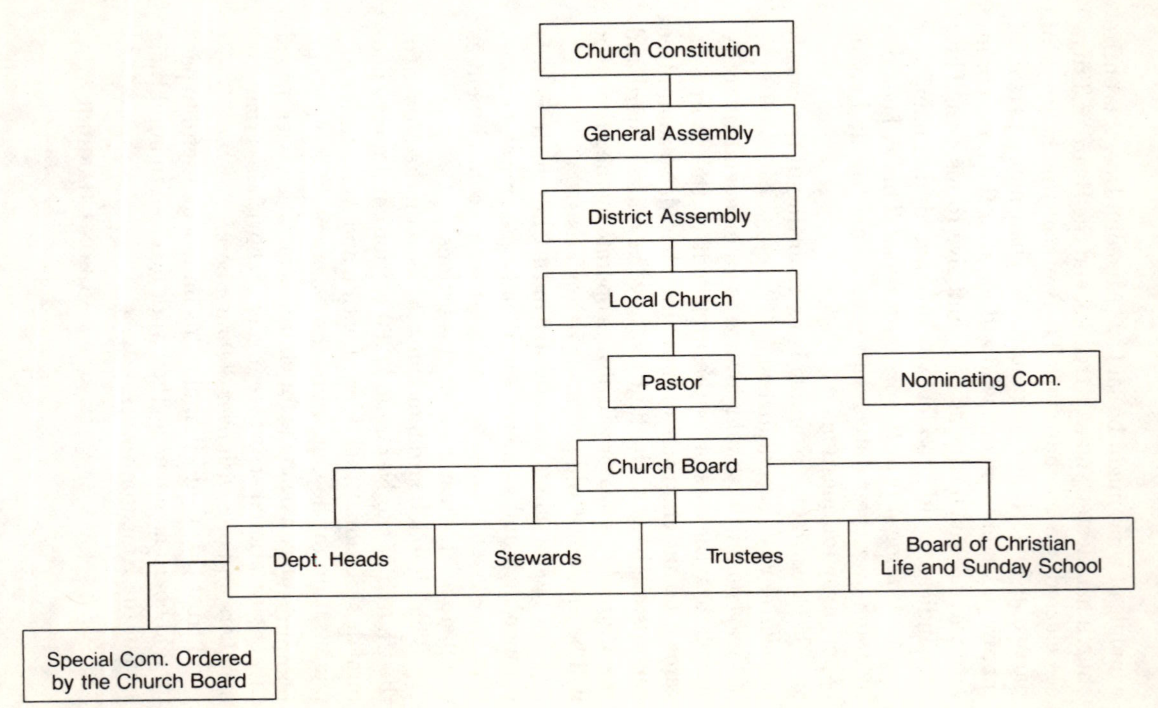

Church Constitution
General Assembly
District Assembly
Local Church
Pastor
Nominating Com.
Church Board
Dept. Heads
Stewards
Trustees
Board of Christian Life and Sunday School
Special Com. Ordered by the Church Board

12

The Meaning of Organization

Organization is the orderly arrangement of tasks in relationship to each other and the establishment of the responsibility of persons for the most effective accomplishment of group goals. It assists each person in knowing his place and function in the life of the church. It is that technique used to harmonize the relationships of people as they work to achieve the institution's goals. Organization makes a oneness and unity from related parts. It is only the organized body that functions as a unit.

It is not hard for the pastor to know if he is leading an organized congregation in purposeful action or if he is working strenuously in an atmosphere of uncertainty. If those selected to carry out a program are not informed of their duties and needless time is spent in repeated explanations; if needed materials are chronically not available at the proper time; if emergencies are constantly arising from a lack of planning; if those in leadership are repeatedly heard to lament, "No one told me," organization is obviously needed.

Many laymen are ready to accept their responsibility for the work of the church, but first they must know what the responsibility is and how it should be discharged. Each task, position, and responsibility must be identified and explained. Organization is never complete until goals have been identified and the people have been given clearly defined tasks that lead toward well-defined goals. The board must feel that "we" set the goals, "we" know our task and the value of the task, "we" understand how the task contributes to the total program of the church, and "we" know how "we" are going to carry it out.

The church board is the servant of the congregation. It exists as a group of chosen leaders to whom the church as a whole can look for planning, coordinating, and evaluating the church's program.

The Church Board

The church is a place of worship foremost, but it also has a business responsibility. The total membership cannot handle all of the details involved in planning, administration, and responsibility for the total church. Therefore, the church *Manual* has provided a church board with committees who will give the time for the detailed study necessary to identify the variety of needs and then perform the assigned tasks.

Purpose

The business of the church board is "to care for the interests of the church and its work, not otherwise provided for, in harmony with the pastor" (136.1).

Developing Official Policies

The church board establishes policies for the smooth operation of the church. The term *policy* is used to mean the formal action of the church board on any affairs of the church organization. Policies may be thought of as the decisions of the church board. Policies are the guidelines for carrying out the church program. All church policies should be in writing. Once a policy is presented and understood by the church personnel, it becomes the duty of each office, person, and department to carry out the decision expressed in the written opinion of the church board. These written policies become the means of organizational control.

Membership

"Every church shall have a church board, composed of the pastor, the chairman of the Board of Christian Life and Sunday School, the president of the Nazarene Youth International, the president of the local Nazarene World Mission Society, the stewards, and the trustees of the church, and the members of the Board of Christian Life and Sunday School when elected as the Education Committee of the church board by the annual church meeting" (134).

Qualifications for Board Members

"We direct our local churches to elect as church officers only persons who are clearly in the experience of entire sanctification; who are in full sympathy with the doctrines, polity, and practices of the Church of the Nazarene; and who support the local church faithfully with tithes and offerings" (38).

Nominating Board Members

Before a person is placed on a ballot, he should know what is expected of him if elected. The following information is a minimum for members of the church board.

1. *Purpose of the board.*

2. *Membership of the board.*

3. *Spiritual qualifications.*

4. *Duties.* Each person should know the designated meeting times, and if the person has a specific duty, he should be well informed. He should be informed concerning the resources that he can expect to help carry out his duties.

Organizing the Church Board

When the board is elected, the pastor, as chairman, should designate the night for the organizing of the board. At that time, the first order of business is to elect a church secretary who shall keep the minutes of the meeting (136.19). A church treasurer is also elected. At this first meeting the Evangelism and Membership Committee should be elected. This committee, along with the trustees, stewards, and Board of Christian Life, which were all elected at the annual meeting, compose the basic standing committees.

Officers

The pastor is chairman, ex officio, of the church board (115.22). Other officers are the church secretary, a church treasurer, and any other officer which it shall be their duty to elect (135).

Duties

1. Care for the financial interests of the church (136.5-36.10), including providing a Counting Committee (136.22), appointing an Auditing Committee (136.23), and electing a treasurer (136.20).

2. Nominate a pastor (136.2).

3. Issue licenses to local preachers, local deaconesses, and recommend same to the District Assembly to become district licensed and for renewal (136.11-36.16). Recommend to the District Assembly persons for director of Christian education (136.25), registered song evangelist (136.26), consecrated deaconess (136.27).

4. Elect paid assistants (136.30).

5. Provide for a church budget, monitoring of the budget, and make a report to the board on this budget (136.5-36.6).

6. Determine pastor's salary and other paid workers and evangelists (136.7-36.9).

Orientation of New Board Members

Time

Studies have shown that there are three possible times that are used most for church board and committee orientation.

1. One night a week is set aside for four to six weeks for training.

2. A special class on the church board is taught in the Sunday School hour.

3. Several church boards from an entire zone come together for one night a week for the training.

Objectives of Orientation

1. Understanding the church government, its aims, programs, district and general relations, and procedures.

2. Understanding the doctrines and history of the church.

3. Acquainting each one with the year's program that has been planned by the previous board.

Each new member should be given a church *Manual*, church year calendar, and a copy of church policies.

Orientation of New Church Officers

Help can and should be given to the new church officers by the pastor and staff by assisting the new officers in getting acquainted with their positions and making them confident and happy in their new duties. The minimum to ensure the success of the new officers would be:

1. *Information.* Be sure that the officers understand their duties and responsibilities.

2. *Satisfaction.* Keep contact in the early days to determine if the officers feel satisfied with their tasks.

3. *Quality.* Determine if the officers have the equipment to do the best job, and evaluate the use of the equipment that the church has.

4. *Reference.* The officers should sufficiently understand the organization of the church so that they know to whom they should go for guidance for the securing of needed materials.

5. *Resources.* They should know about the church resources and their locations. This should include both the materials and human resources.

6. *Emphasis.* Foremost in all church work is the emphasis that each job is for the building of the kingdom of God. If a board member feels that he is not doing an acceptable task, there will be a sense of defeat. This will rob the person of needed enthusiasm and vision.

Motivation

Motivation can occur only with the following:

1. They must know their duties.

2. They must know how to carry out these duties.

3. They must have the information needed to act intelligently.

4. They must be recognized for work well done.

Authority

The fact should be well established that all legal authority is vested in the board as a corporate body. Therefore, this body can only act at an authorized meeting duly called. Whether a member of the board acts separately, or if all members of the board act in agreement but the decision was *not* made in a duly called board meeting with opportunity for counsel, such action would be without authority (legal meeting, 135). The Church of the Nazarene has a constitutional form of government; therefore, all action of the board must be in harmony with the established law of the church.

Accepted Order of Business

1. Call to order
2. Reading of minutes of the previous meeting
3. Treasurer's report
4. Reports of standing committees
5. Reports of special committees
6. Unfinished business
7. New business
8. Announcements
9. Adjournment

Church Board Committees

A committee is a small group of church members elected or appointed to perform certain clearly identified tasks for a stated period of time. The church elects the church board, and the church board determines any additional committees that may be needed and determines their membership and duties. Each committee must answer to the church board.

The Value of Church Board Committees

A committee can function more effectively than a large group to help the church accomplish its basic goals and objectives. There are several reasons that make this true:

1. *Discussion.* The discussion is less formal. Everyone has better opportunity to participate. There is even room for friendly disagreement. The interaction stimulates thinking. Because they can speak up freely, there is more interest. The small group offers a better opportunity to talk out issues and thereby give opportunity to reconcile differences.

2. *Duties.* Committee duties are more specific. The church board studies the total church program while committees specialize. This gives opportunity for detailed study that assists them in arriving at some specifics that are in turn recommended to the church board. Better use can be made of the knowledge of authorities in their fields.

3. *Committee meetings.* They save the time of the church board by meeting preceding the board meeting. They carefully research a problem and compile their data into a report. They come to the board meeting with a recommendation for action. This helps the orderly operation of the board.

4. *A sense of responsibility.* Knowing that one's committee is responsible for specific areas of the church and the church body or board has elected them for that duty brings a sense of personal responsibility. The committee members will experience personal growth as they share in the purposeful work of the church.

5. *Time.* The committee can give a longer time to its specialty than the total board can. Each subject is evaluated, solutions are studied, and the best solution is recommended to the church board. Opportunity can be given for non-committee members or non-board members to share information with them.

Types of Committees

1. *Special committees.* These committees are appointed by the church board to perform some specific task; and when this task is completed and the final report is submitted to the church board, the committee ceases to exist. For example, a committee to choose carpet for the church.

2. *Regular committees.* These are standing committees chosen to perform tasks in a specific field over the assembly year. For example, trustees.

The board should seek to keep its number of committees to a minimum. It is a good rule to refer most board duties to a standing committee whenever possible.

Determining the Need for Committees

The *Manual* states that each church shall have trustees, stewards, and a Board of Christian Life (134), and an Evangelism and Church Membership Committee (109).

Before a special committee is called for, the church board should answer the following questions:

1. Can a special committee gather pertinent facts better than an existing one?

2. Will a special committee interfere with a standing committee's work?

If the first question cannot be answered with a yes and the second no, a special committee is not needed. Remember, the rule is to work through standing committees as often as possible.

If it has been determined that a special committee is needed, the following procedure should be taken. The board should determine: (1) the number that should be on the committee, (2) how the members shall be elected or appointed, (3) what special qualifications will be needed for each member, and (4) the date to receive the report from the special committee.

If the board votes for the chairman to appoint the committee, he is confronted with a delicate problem. Shall he choose close friends, those with common views or divergent views, influential people or some influential? Will he choose only those with special knowledge of the problem?

It is well known that a committee of uninformed people can do no more than share their lack of knowledge. It will be necessary for some of the committee to be capable people, or competent work cannot be expected.

Most organizations find it an advantage to have a standing Nominating Committee that can present the names to the board for their approval. There are three major factors to be considered in each individual's nomination. Each person nominated should be chosen mainly on the basis of the contribution they can make (1) as a Christian example, (2) as one possessing specific abilities in the area of assignment, and (3) in being willing to serve throughout the life of the committee.

The Committee Chairman

The committee chairman is to plan and guide the committee in the achievement of the tasks assigned to it. If the committee is to be successful, the committee chairman must carry out the following:

1. *Prepare an agenda.* Typically the agenda (order of business) will be as follows:

   a. Call the meeting to order. When the time has come for the meeting to begin, the chairman will start with "The meeting will come to order. Mr. John Doe, will you open the meeting with prayer?"

   b. Call for the reading of the minutes of the previous meeting. The chairman should ask, "Will the secretary read the minutes of the previous meeting?"

   c. Call for the report of any committee or subcommittee that has been assigned to make a study.

   d. Call for unfinished business. The chairman may question, "Mr. Secretary, do we have any unfinished business?"

   e. Call for new business. The chairman may declare, "The chair will receive any new business." If some member of the board addresses the chair, the chairman will answer, "Mr. John Doe has the floor." When a motion has been made, the chairman will confirm, "You have heard the motion [here it is often wise to repeat the motion]. Is there a second?" No motion should be considered without a second.

f. Adjournment. A member of the committee will make a motion, "I move that we adjourn." The chairman will respond, "The motion is made that we adjourn. All in favor say aye. Those opposed say no. The motion is carried. We are adjourned."

The purpose of the agenda is not to be formal, but to prevent a loss of time, to be democratic, to give everyone the opportunity to speak, and to be fair.

2. *The courteous chairman* presides with the following in mind:

a. People are more important than procedure.

b. The church board meeting is to be Christlike more than businesslike.

c. He is to be courteous at all times and with all people, protect the rights of the timid, and never embarrass anyone if they are in error.

d. The chairman is to be neutral. He can give information; he can state, "A motion is in order to ______"; but he should never make a motion.

e. The wise leader makes it a principle that good creative discussion is in order. He is alert to lead members to talk through their disagreements.

f. A good chairman recognizes a member who has not spoken. By giving him preference over one who has spoken, he will alternate discussion so as to bring out both sides of a question.

The Committee Secretary

The secretary should keep complete notes of the committee meeting so that an accurate record of the committee's discussion are recorded. These should be given to the church board secretary so that they become a part of the permanent church files.

Training Committee Members

It is a fact that committee members cannot do any better than they know to do. Therefore, an annual training session for church committee members and chairmen is needed. The church board should meet as a committee of the whole. Their duties, procedures, and time of meeting should be discussed in the first meeting.

The following objectives of leadership training are agreed upon:

1. To assist the laymen to increase theirs and the congregation's knowledgeable participation in church administration.

2. To assist the church board and congregation in understanding the meaning and purpose of the church.

3. There should be a clear understanding of the resources that are available to them.

4. A place should be provided for their meetings.

5. Clear instructions are to be given as to what is expected of them in the way of objectives, procedures, and deadlines.

Standing Committees

Standing committees (regular committees as opposed to special committees) are chosen to perform tasks in a specific field over the assembly year.

Board of Trustees

Membership

Elected by ballot at the annual church meeting

Meetings

Monthly or on call

Manual Duties

1. Hold the titles to church properties (exceptions, 150.1).

2. Serve as a long-range planning committee.

3. Give guidance to the development of the physical facilities and financial planning (exceptions, 150.3).

4. Be amenable to the church board.

Church Board Assigned Duties

1. Insurance
   a. All church properties are to be insured in light of up-to-date appraisals.
   b. See that insurance policies are paid by a studied plan and that said policies are kept with the

record of holdings (pianos, pews, etc.) in a safe place.

2. Care
   a. Develop a job description for the custodian.
   b. Develop a checklist for weekly inspection of the custodian's effectiveness.
   c. See that buildings and equipment are in good repair by a scheduled check of the following:
      (1) Outside
          (a) Sidewalks
          (b) Drives
          (c) Lawn
          (d) Shrubbery
          (e) Parking Area
      (2) Exterior of buildings
          (a) Roofs
          (b) Walls
          (c) Windows
          (d) Outdoor signs
          (e) Outdoor lights
      (3) Sanctuary
          (a) Walls (wet spots)
          (b) Ceiling (leaks)
          (c) Lighting
          (d) Speaker system
          (e) Windows and doors
          (f) Pews
          (g) Flooring
          (h) Organ and piano
          (i) Baptismal equipment
          (j) Heating and air conditioning (check filter regularly)
      (4) Educational units
          (a) Walls and ceilings

        (b) Windows, curtains, and blinds
        (c) Chairs and tables
        (d) Pianos
        (e) Nursery equipment
    (5) Fellowship unit
        (a) Kitchen and equipment
        (b) Dining room
        (c) Tables and chairs
    (6) Washrooms
        (a) Walls and floors
        (b) Lights
        (c) Mirrors
        (d) Study of needs
    (7) Wiring and lighting
        (a) Bulbs
        (b) Wall switches
        (c) Wires

3. Equipment Inspection

All guarantees should be kept by the church secretary. The trustees should supervise the maintenance of the equipment according to instructions. Prepare a budget for expected replacements.

4. Supervise Custodian
  a. Weekly checklist
  b. Check storage room. All flammables should be kept in fireproof metal containers.

5. Key Policy
  a. No key is to be made or issued without approval of the trustees.
  b. A record of all keys is to be kept by the trustees.
  c. A set of duplicate keys to all locks shall be labeled, tagged, and under the care of the chairman of the trustees.

d. The number of keys in circulation shall be kept to a minimum.

e. Employees or elected officers shall surrender their keys promptly when there is a change in employment or office positions.

6. Inventory

An inventory shall include a listing, cost, and date of purchase or, if a gift, the fair market value of all church holdings:

a. Equipment: Typewriters, mimeograph, projectors, and other such holdings.

b. Furnishings: Pews, chairs, tables, desks, rugs, chalkboards, nursery equipment, and other such holdings.

c. Supplies: One person shall be appointed to keep a record of all purchases.

7. Parsonage

The minister cares for the house in which he lives and makes requests for repairs or new facilities as the need may arise. Even so, the parsonage does belong to the church, and the trustees should keep in mind that the church is responsible for the maintenance of it as duly cared-for church property in the following areas:

a. Roof

b. Paint

c. Heating and cooling

d. Electric wiring

e. Plumbing

f. Appliances furnished

g. Shrubbery

h. Insurance

Membership

Elected by ballot at the annual church meeting

Meetings

Monthly or on call

Manual Duties (144-46)

1. Raise money for church needs.

2. Provide for the Lord's Supper.

3. Care for the needy of the church.

4. Aid in making available Christian service opportunities to all members.

Church Board Assigned Duties

Stewards serve as Worship Committee, Music Committee, and Communion Committee and, as such, are responsible for services, sacraments, music, and ushering.

1. Worship Committee Duties
   a. Consult with the pastor and minister of music in developing the best possible worship service.
   b. Help to watch for any congregational behavior that is distracting. (Talking or unnecessary going in and out.)
   c. Observations that can be helpful:
      (1) Is the service Christ-centered?
      (2) Is the total service united in a harmonious oneness?
      (3) Do the minister and minister of music leave the pulpit on errands after the service begins?
      (4) Does the minister or minister of music do any unnecessary talking?

(5) Does the service have order, movement, and climax?

(6) Is the offering worshipful?

2. Music Committee Duties

The stewards as the Music Committee are the link between the congregation and the music program of the church.

a. The minister of music should keep a record of the hymns used, should do no unnecessary talking, and should wear clothing that is appropriate for the service.

b. The Music Committee should consult with the minister of music in making the service worshipful.

c. The people should have an opportunity to express praise through participation in singing.

d. There should be a music budget adequate for the church music program.

e. The minister of music should be in control of the choir and music program.

f. The music should show evidence of being well prepared.

g. The church should develop a well-organized music library. Elect a competent choir member as music librarian.

h. Music should not be taken from the church without permission of the minister of music or music librarian.

i. All special songs should be planned two weeks in advance and practiced adequately for presentation.

3. Communion Committee Duties

The minister and Communion Committee should strive for neatness and orderliness in the service.

a. Trays, glasses, bread and grape juice, clean table-cloths, and a cloth to cover the elements should be obtained.

b. See that all participants are well instructed before the service.

c. The table should be prepared in its entirety before the people arrive for the service.

d. Assist the minister in seeing that the sick and shut-ins are provided the Lord's Supper regularly. The Communion is often more meaningful for the shut-ins if members of this committee accompany the pastor.

e. The trays, glasses, and unused bread and grape juice should be covered immediately upon the completion of Communion being served.

The Board of Christian Life and Sunday School

Membership

Elected by ballot at the annual church meeting.

Meetings

Monthly or on call.

***Manual* Duties** (157.1-57.14)

1. Make one or more nominations approved by the pastor to the annual church meeting for chairman of the Board of Christian Life (157.4).

2. State the purpose and evaluate effectiveness of programs in attaining the purpose.

3. Evaluate curriculum materials to insure maximum benefit is being received from money spent. Recommend materials needed for the best teaching.

4. Survey the educational needs of the church at the beginning of each church year.

5. Work with the pastor and Christian Life chairman in the selection of teachers and officers (157.5, 157.7).

6. Make recommendations to the church board where educational problems are involved.

7. Coordinate the work of all educational programs of the church.

8. Be responsible for departmental organization.

9. Work with youth leaders in development of programs.

10. Develop and offer a teacher training program.

11. Set dates for the meeting of department heads.

12. Study teacher qualifications of all teachers.

13. Nominate church librarian to church board and, with librarian, evaluate and recommend new materials.

14. Be responsible for nursery.

Nominating Committee

Purpose

This committee's duty is to select and present the names of nominees for positions to be filled.

Personnel

Three or more persons are to be chosen by the church board.

Organization

The pastor shall serve as chairman (112.10). A secretary shall be elected.

Duties

1. Select, interview, and present names of those to be voted on.

2. Assist the church board and church meetings in discovering and enlisting qualified, spiritual, and talented persons for positions.

3. Prepare ballot for elections.

4. Organize boards of tellers for elections.

Finance Committee

Purpose

They shall have the management and supervision of all financial affairs of the church. They shall answer to the church board for these duties by making monthly reports to the church board pertaining to the financial status of the church.

Personnel

There shall be no fewer than five members elected by the church board to serve for the next church year and until their successors have been elected. The treasurer and financial secretary shall be members ex officio. The pastor is the chairman. An associate chairman shall be elected by the Finance Committee.

Organization

The pastor is the chairman. The Finance Committee shall elect an associate chairman. The financial secretary shall act as secretary of the committee.

Duties

1. Organize the total financial program of the church.

2. Evaluate the present and potential giving of the church.

3. Give supervision and oversee the financial affairs of the church and all of its departments.

4. Study and approve the collection and expenditures of all church funds.

5. Approve the systems of accounts used by the treasurer and financial secretary.

6. Approve the system for handling offerings, counting, and handling of offering envelopes; and, with the financial secretary, be responsible for counters.

7. Keep an ongoing study to insure proper safeguards for all church moneys and to insure that the church shall be in a sound financial condition.

8. Report monthly to the church board.

9. Present a church budget to the church board one month preceding the end of the church year.

10. Establish the timetable for all programs in the church budget.

11. Develop and recommend ways of handling unforeseen financial needs.

Handling Cash Receipts

The Finance Committee is responsible for the handling of all cash receipts by the following approved procedures.

1. Two or more persons should take the offerings to the church office.

2. When the money is counted, more than one person is to be involved. This is required by the church *Manual.*

3. As each envelope is opened and counted, compare the cash count with the amount written on it. If a slight difference occurs, change the amount on the envelope to

harmonize with the money in the envelope. If a large discrepancy is found, notify the contributor.

4. When all the money from the envelopes has been recorded and totaled, total the amount recorded on the envelopes, and check to see if the two totals are the same.

5. Record the amount of all known contributors on the prepared forms. These records should be updated weekly.

6. The empty envelopes should never leave the church office. The financial secretary or the person designated should be responsible for them. These records are private and should be kept under lock.

Disbursement of Money

The Finance Committee is responsible for the execution of the board policy of disbursing money. The following should be observed:

1. No money is to be spent without authorization of the church board.

2. Items that occur regularly should have the standing permission of the church board.

3. Items that occur irregularly but are necessary may be paid by a signed purchase order from a department head or the chairman of the Finance Committee. (The church board must set the policy.)

4. Special orders that exceed $100 must have the approval of the church board.

The Treasurer's Relationship to the Finance Committee

The treasurer is an officer of the church board but works with the Finance Committee. The Finance Committee's policies that have been approved by the church board relating to the treasurer are as follows:

1. The handling of funds is not the duty of the treasurer.

2. Each check that is signed must also have a record that will make it possible for him to prepare his reports.

3. All records must be kept current.

4. His books must be balanced with the bank each month.

5. Checks are not to be written if they have not been properly authorized.

6. A file for receipts, expenditures, and needed records should be kept for future reference.

7. Church moneys are to be expended in accordance with the church board policies.

8. He is to give a monthly report of expenditures and report the status of the treasury.

Evangelism and Membership Committee

Purpose

The Evangelism and Membership Committee acts in the capacity of an advisory committee to the pastor. It shall be the duty of this committee to conserve the fruits of evangelism (109-9.1).

Personnel

This committee is made up of not fewer than three persons (109) provided by the church board. The members of this committee should be known for their mature Christian experience, good judgment, ability to inspire confidence, and the ability to express themselves tactfully.

Organization

The pastor is the chairman. A secretary should be

elected and records kept carefully for the report to the church board.

Duties

1. Urge new converts to qualify for church membership by a consistent devotional life and a study of the Bible and the *Manual* (109.4).

2. Assist the pastor in quarterly church membership classes. When needed, visit in the homes so that prospective members may be advised and instructed in the doctrines and rules of the church.

3. This committee should be as active in visiting dropouts as in bringing in new members. After new members are received, the committee shall work with the pastor in developing a continued program of spiritual guidance.

Meetings

This committee shall meet when called by the pastor.

Special Church Board Officer

Financial Secretary

Duties

1. Be responsible to receive and be custodian of the church offering envelopes.

2. Keep records and be able to document moneys received.

3. Be responsible to record giving of each individual account.

4. Give to each contributor a yearly report of his contributions.

5. Give to the treasurer a copy of the deposit ticket prepared by the counting committee.

Policies

Policies may be thought of as the decisions of the church board. These policies are established for the smooth operation of the church. They are made by the *formal* action of the church board. They are the guidelines for carrying out the church program. Once a policy is presented and understood by the church personnel, it becomes the duty of each office, person, and department to carry out the policies.

All church policies should be in writing. Policy making is an ongoing activity of the church board.

Nursery

The nursery is under the supervision of the Board of Christian Life and Sunday School and through this board answers to the church board. Careful work by the committee insures a uniformly high quality of care each time a nursery child comes to the church as well as providing a more effective ministry to the parents of the nursery children.

The attendant in charge, whether employed or not, must be approved and any salary set by the church board.

The attendant in charge should present any financial needs to the chairman of the Education Committee.

Duties

1. The attendant in charge should make recommendations about cleanliness and care of the nursery rooms.

2. The nursery rooms should be cleaned regularly and toys should be sterilized after each use. (Use a solution of Zephiran Chloride concentrate: two tablespoons to one gallon of water.)

3. Beds should be cleaned after each session.

4. When assistants are used, they are to be selected by the attendant in charge and should be rotated. No one under 18 should be used.

5. The toy box should be locked at all times when the children are present.

6. No one should be in the nursery who has not been invited in by the attendant in charge.

7. Only the parents, or the one bringing the child, should come to the nursery to pick the child up.

8. The children are to be handed to the attendant over the door. Children will be picked up in the same manner. The bottom half of the door will remain locked at all times.

9. Before any item is given or brought to the nursery, it must be approved by the Education Committee. The following questions must be answered: (1) Does the nursery have use for it? (2) Is it safe? (3) Is it sturdy? Any item donated must be given without restraints.

10. Board sets age limitations at three years and under.

11. The child's name should be affixed on all bottles, diapers, and so on.

12. Nursery hours should be for regular services and other services set by the board.

13. Health requirements: Attendant in charge should wear a smock, change the sheets between all services, and ask that no going in and out should be done by non-nursery attendants.

14. The attendant in charge makes regular reports to the Christian Education Committee.

15. After a child has been accepted in the nursery, the attendant in charge should not leave the rooms. The church could be held liable.

Custodian

Terms

Terms of employment, hours, salary, vacation, and special services with extra pay (such as revivals and weddings) are set by the board.

Principal Functions

Keep the physical property clean, comfortable, and orderly, and report to the trustees any needed repairs.

Regular Duties

1. Vacuum or sweep, clean, and dust offices.

2. Vacuum, clean, and dust nursery after each day of use.

3. Vacuum or sweep, clean, and dust all other parts of the building.

4. Scrub, wax, and polish all floors where needed, according to schedule or as often as needed.

5. Clean all rest rooms and replenish all supplies weekly.

6. Arrange all tables, chairs, and other equipment as directed by teachers or trustees.

7. Clean and polish taps or drinking fountains weekly.

8. Curtains and draperies that are torn or unclean should be reported to trustees.

9. Maps, teaching stands, and chalkboards should be in proper place. Clean as needed.

10. Old posters, books, and paper should be removed. (When in question report to trustees.)

11. Flammables should be stored in closed containers.

Cleaning Checklist on Custodial Work

To be checked by trustees each week after cleaning is complete. Check, sign, and date.

1. Empty wastebaskets
2. Dust sanctuary
3. Dust educational unit
4. See that classrooms are in order
5. Clean toilets
6. Clean urinals
7. Clean washbasins
8. Supply toilet tissue
9. Supply towel boxes
10. Supply soap
11. Dust mop all floors (where appropriate)
12. Clean drinking fountains
13. Vacuum nursery floors
14. Clean nursery
15. Vacuum carpet
16. Arrange songbooks
17. Report needed supplies
18. Report needed repairs to trustees

Name ____

Date ____

Courtesy Committee

Responsibilities

    1. Meet as needed.

    2. Have jurisdiction over any part of the church that is used for special purposes. Keep calendar free from conflicting dates.

    3. In charge of church equipment for special purposes.

    4. Take care of any needs regarding flowers to the ill and where there is a death, food where there is a death, and any other special needs. There should be no duplications with church departments.

    5. Investigate all requests for help. If the request is deemed valid, communicate the need to the Finance Committee.

    6. Responsible for showers, gifts, or other events of a social nature that represents the church.

    7. Determine policies that are needed relative to flowers, food, gifts, showers, and other services. These should be approved by the church board. (Policy should state "For members, regular attenders, and their immediate families.")

Church Property

It should be the policy of the church board that any and all uses of church property must receive the approval of the trustees.

Areas Where Policies Are Needed

    1. Church physical equipment such as musical instruments, use of the nursery, audiovisual equipment, dining facilities, church van, and so on.

2. Finance, such as budgets, purchasing, insurance, and so on.

3. Personnel, such as housing, vacations, insurance, and so on.

The following is an example of a policy on the use of the church van.

The driver of the church van may be held personally liable for injuries growing out of negligence. Therefore, it is the policy of the church board that any and all uses of the church van must receive the approval of the trustees. The driver of the church van must receive the approval of the trustees and be approved by the church's insurance company.

Committee Activities

In the church office each church officer and committee chairperson has a mailbox. When anyone in the church feels that a department head, a church officer, or a committee chairperson needs information on a subject or that there is a problem that needs attention, they have a place to take this information. The church office secretary places it in the appropriate box. Having input is rewarding.

The department heads can refer any needs to the proper committee, and the committee refers it to the church board with their recommendations.

The committees meet immediately following the church board meeting. This gives them an opportunity to begin consideration of all materials referred to them by the church board. By the next board meeting they have had time for evaluation and are prepared to give their report.

Following is a report from a newly elected Board of Trustees with a newly elected chairperson. The report shows action taken from the previous board meeting and presents recommendations for future action.

Report of Board of Trustees

Earnest Etheridge, Chairman

June 4, 1984

The following have been completed:

   1. Shrubbery planted at the parsonage: $128.50.

2. Parsonage shutters attached and painted: $187.94.

3. One air conditioner in the sanctuary reworked.

4. One air conditioner installed in the chapel.

5. One light fixture installed at church entrance: $35.00.

NOTE: A total of $351.44 has been spent.

The following are recommended:

1. Replace the wood and repaint eight windows: $75.00.

2. Rework carpet in the center hall: $100.00.

3. Replace four pieces of 4 x 6 ceiling tile in the hall in front of the Sunday School office: $40.00.

4. Repair water closet in the nursery and purchase some new toys: $100.00.

5. Cornice work needed on the outside.

6. Four lights needed in the chapel: $120.00.

7. Replace baseboards in the center hall.

8. Two gallons of varnish needed for doors and baseboards in the hallways.

9. Fence needs to be cleaned on east side of church property.

10. Installation of bath fixtures and showers and work on the ball goals in family life center.

11. Additional wall plugs needed in the church office.

12. Work needs to begin as soon as possible on the family life center.

NOTE: A total of not less than $535.00 is needed to accomplish the above goals.